THE U.S.A. in pictures

By Dr. STANLEY N. MILLER,
PROFESSOR OF SOCIAL SCIENCE AND EDUCATION,
PENNSYLVANIA STATE UNIVERSITY,
and RUTH V. NOBLE

Pike's Peak. "Purple mountain majesty above the fruited plain."

 STERLING PUBLISHING CO., INC. NEW YORK

Oak Tree Press Co., Ltd. London & Sydney

VISUAL GEOGRAPHY SERIES

Afghanistan
Alaska
Argentina
Australia
Austria
Belgium and Luxembourg
Berlin—East and West
Bolivia
Brazil
Bulgaria
Canada
The Caribbean (English-
　Speaking Islands)
Ceylon (Sri Lanka)
Chile
China
Colombia
Costa Rica
Cuba
Czechoslovakia
Denmark
Ecuador
Egypt
El Salvador
England

Ethiopia
Fiji
Finland
France
French Canada
Ghana
Greece
Greenland
Guatemala
Haiti
Hawaii
Holland
Honduras
Hong Kong
Hungary
Iceland
India
Indonesia
Iran
Iraq
Ireland
Islands of the
　Mediterranean
Israel
Italy

Jamaica
Japan
Jordan
Kenya
Korea
Kuwait
Lebanon
Liberia
Madagascar (Malagasy)
Malawi
Malaysia and Singapore
Mexico
Morocco
Nepal
New Zealand
Nicaragua
Norway
Pakistan and Bangladesh
Panama and the Canal
　Zone
Peru
The Philippines
Poland
Portugal
Puerto Rico

Rhodesia
Rumania
Russia
Saudi Arabia
Scotland
Senegal
South Africa
Spain
Surinam
Sweden
Switzerland
Tahiti and the
　French Islands of
　the Pacific
Taiwan
Tanzania
Thailand
Tunisia
Turkey
Uruguay
The U.S.A.
Venezuela
Wales
West Germany
Yugoslavia

PICTURE CREDITS

The publisher wishes to thank the following for supplying photographs used in this book: Agency of Development & Community Affairs, Montpelier, Vermont; American Hereford Association; California Office of Tourism, Sacramento, California; Cape Cod Chamber of Commerce, Hyannis, Massachusetts; Chesapeake and Ohio Railway Co., Cleveland, Ohio; Coca Cola Co., New York, New York; Colorado Travel Section, Denver, Colorado; Currier & Ives; Department of Economic Development; Eastern Airlines, New York; Environmental Science Services Administration; Fay Foto Service, Boston, Massachusetts; Fisher Body; Library of Congress, Washington, D.C.; Florida State News Bureau; Robert C. Forsyth; Greater Boston Chamber of Commerce, Boston, Massachusetts; Elizabeth Hibbs; Howard Johnson's Restaurants, Braintree, Massachusetts; Iowa Development Commission; Kentucky Department of Public Information, Frankfort, Kentucky; Kentucky Fried Chicken, Yonkers, New York; Levitt & Sons—Strathmore Glen, Glen Cove, N.Y.; Louisiana Tourist Development Commission, Baton Rouge, Louisiana; McDonald's Hamburgers, Englewood Cliffs, New Jersey; Maine Department of Commerce and Industry; Massachusetts Dept. of Commerce and Development Division of Tourism, Boston, Massachusetts; Missouri Tourism Commission, Jefferson City, Missouri; Museum of Science, Boston, Massachusetts; NASA; Nathan's Famous, New York; National Gallery of Art, Washington, D.C.; National Park Service; New York State Department of Commerce; Pan American Airways; Pennsylvania Department of Commerce, Harrisburg, Pennsylvania; San Francisco Convention & Visitors Bureau; Santa Fe Railway; Southern California Visitors Council, Los Angeles, California; Standard Oil Co. (N.J.); Tropicana Productions, Bradenton, Florida; Union Pacific Railroad; UPI Photo; U.S. Army Photograph; USIA, New York; Utah Travel Council (Ramon Winegar), Salt Lake City, Utah; University of California, Berkeley, California; Virginia Department of Conservation & Economic Development, Richmond, Virginia; Virginia State Travel Service, Richmond, Virginia; Walt Disney Productions, Washington Area Convention and Visitors Bureau, Washington, D.C.; West Penn Power Co., Greensburg, Pennsylvania; West Virginia Department of Commerce, Charleston, West Virginia. Acknowledgement is also given to the following books published by Sterling Publishing Co. from which illustrations were used: "Cars in Pictures"; "Curiosities of Animal Life"; "Fifty-One Capitals of the U.S.A."; "Fresh Look at American History" series; "Government at Work."

CONTENTS

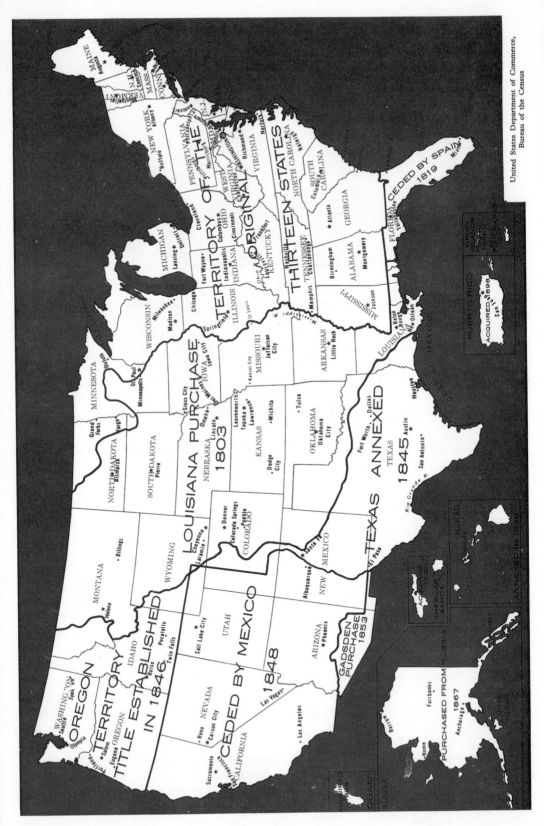

United States Department of Commerce,
Bureau of the Census

4

Highland Light at Truro, Massachusetts, near the tip of Cape Cod where it curves like an elbow into the Atlantic Ocean. One of the most powerful lights on the Atlantic coast, it may be seen twenty miles at sea.

I. THE LAND

A VAST AREA of diverse topographical and climatic conditions, the United States of America, with 50 states, is the fourth largest country both in population (1970 census: 203,235,298) and in area (3,615,122 sq. mi. or 9,399,317 sq. km.). Located in the middle of the North American continent, it stretches over 3,000 miles (4,800 km.) from the Atlantic to the Pacific Ocean, bordered by Canada on the north, and Mexico and the Gulf of Mexico on the south. Westward, off the Pacific coast, across 2,397 miles (3,835 km.) of ocean lies the state of Hawaii, a group of 5 major and many smaller islands. Alaska to the northwest, the other non-contiguous state, is separated from the rest of the nation by western Canada. Westward from the Atlantic coast, the coastal plain and Appalachian Mountains of the East and then the prairies of the wide Midwest give way to the sharp peaks of the Rocky Mountains that cut the country longitudinally from Canada to

Mexico. Extremes of climate range from the subtropical temperatures of southern Florida to the icy blizzards of the upper Midwest.

The land of the U.S.A. is endowed with a wealth of natural resources which has enabled an energetic people to make the country into the richest in the world with the highest standard of living. The country is blessed with large areas of fertile land used for the growing of crops and the grazing of animals. Along the coasts, fishing is an important industry. Rich mineral deposits are located primarily in the highlands of the East and West in combinations useful for manufacturing. Iron ore, located in the upper Midwest and coal mined in the Appalachian highlands, form the foundation for the heavy industry of the manufacturing belt that stretches from the northeast coast to Chicago, in the heart of the Midwest.

This land of diverse geographical features can be divided into four large regions.

The potato crop is second only to timber in Maine, which is one of the three largest potato producing states in the U.S.A. The fields of Aroostook and nearby counties are beautiful when the potatoes are in bloom.

THE NORTHEAST

Draw a line from the northern tip of Maine along the Canadian frontier, down the Atlantic coast to the Potomac River that separates Washington, D.C. from Virginia, then westward around Maryland across West Virginia to the Ohio line, now northward around Pennsylvania and New York State, across the top of Vermont and New Hampshire and back around Maine— and you have outlined what is generally regarded as the Northeast, including New England.

It is the smallest region in the U.S.A. (6 per cent of the total area), but it supports one quarter of the U.S. people.

New England's six states (Maine, New Hampshire, Vermont, Massachusetts, Rhode Island and Connecticut) have been completely glaciated, and are dominated by rolling hills and scarped mountains with a general elevation of 2,000 feet (680 m.). The highest uplands occur in the Green Mountains of Vermont and the White Mountains of New Hampshire, where a few rugged peaks reach an altitude over 5,000 feet (1,500 m.). Major lowlands include the valleys of the Merrimack, Housatonic and Connecticut Rivers, the Lake Champlain trench,

the Narragansett, Portland and Boston basins, and the Aroostook Valley in Maine. Early single industry settlements in these valleys still remain and retain the traditions of their ancestors.

The Appalachian Mountain chain forms a

Considered one of the most beautiful of New England churches, this one in Bennington, Vermont, built in the early 1800's, is typical of many others that dominate village greens in almost every New England town.

The new style in government office buildings is typical of these in Boston, which are surrounded by many old historic buildings, such as Faneuil Hall and the Old State House.

highland barrier which extends from Maine southwest to Alabama. The northeastern part of it includes the Shenandoah Ridge and Valley area, as well as the Allegheny Front. Although sparsely populated, this highland area with its many lakes and waterfalls left by the glaciers, is a popular summer and winter playground for the people of nearby urban areas.

An almost continuous 500-mile (850-km.) line of cities and urban developments runs from Boston to Washington, D.C., and is referred to as a "megalopolis" or aggregation of metropolitan areas. All the major cities are port cities, except Washington.

Boston (641,000), capital of Massachusetts and one of the oldest cities of the nation, retains much of the tradition of early New England.

Streets are narrow and crooked and in many areas the architecture mixes the old and the new. The city and its suburbs are renowned for a fine literary tradition, numerous universities and technological research institutions.

King's Chapel, here silhouetted against the more modern Parker House hotel, is one of the most historic churches of Boston, Massachusetts. To the left is the old burying ground which contains many Pilgrims, such as Governor John Winthrop and Reverend John Cotton.

Brooklyn Bridge is one of a series of bridges connecting Manhattan Island to the other boroughs of New York City. The limited space on Manhattan forced the city to expand upward, creating its celebrated skyline which is beautiful at almost any time of day. More than 16,000,000 visitors pour in every year, making New York the country's most popular tourist spot.

New York (7,895,000), the largest city in the U.S.A. and home of the United Nations Organization, started to outgrow the others because of the construction of the Erie Canal in the 1820's and the rail systems that connected its fine port to the hinterland. The greater New York area sprawls over three islands, Manhattan, Staten, and Long, and part of the mainland. Manhattan Island is best known for its gigantic skyscrapers that house many of the leading financial, industrial, and commercial firms of the nation. The city dominates banking, insurance, and investments, leads the country in production and styling of clothes, controls much of the manufacturing of books and periodicals, and is the hub of the country's theatrical and musical enterprises. New York City is divided into five boroughs: Manhattan (contiguous with the island), the Bronx (part of the mainland), Brooklyn and Queens (which are part of Long Island) and Richmond (Staten Island). People

Flags decorate the First Avenue entrance to the United Nations Headquarters in mid-Manhattan on the East River. The massive Secretariat Building at the right dominates the complex; there the staff work is performed. The General Assembly, where important debates are often held, meets for about 14 weeks, beginning in mid-September.

Independence Hall in Philadelphia is where the Declaration of Independence was signed and the Constitution adopted. Here, too, Washington accepted the role of Commander-in-Chief of the Continental Army. The famous Liberty Bell and inkstand used by the signers of the Declaration of Independence are on display here.

emigrated from all over the world to inhabit, first, ethnic pockets in the city, and then to spread out and live all over the city and the metropolitan area, including Long Island, Westchester County to the north, Connecticut and nearby New Jersey.

Philadelphia, Pennsylvania (1,950,000) was developed according to a plan laid out by William Penn in 1682. The central city forms the business district with a gridiron pattern of streets extending outwards. Many of America's historical shrines are located in Philadelphia, including Independence Hall, with the Liberty Bell; Carpenter's Hall, and the Betsy Ross House. The city has many park areas that were laid out by its original planners.

Baltimore, Maryland (906,000) is located 150 miles (240 km.) north of the entrance from the Atlantic to Chesapeake Bay. The city is pri-

The Germans of Pennsylvania, popularly called Pennsylvania Dutch, still carry on the traditions of their forefathers of a century ago. The Amish, especially, are noted for their plain, uniform style of dress and for their use of the horse and buggy for transportation. In this typical scene, a father and son drive past a one-room schoolhouse which is still in use today. This sect is found in Lancaster and other sections of southeastern Pennsylvania and in Ohio and Kansas.

The oldest (1792) public building in Washington, the White House, residence of the President, was designed by an Irish-born architect, James Hoban, who modelled it on the Duke of Leinster's house in Dublin.

Mount Vernon, home of George Washington, overlooks the Potomac River in Virginia, near Washington, D.C. Here Washington lived the life of a prosperous country squire until he left to lead the Continental Army. He returned after his second term as President, died here in 1799, and is buried on the estate. The gardens and grounds, open to visitors, are substantially as he designed them.

The John F. Kennedy Center for the Performing Arts, on the bank of the Potomac River in Washington, D.C., has two theatres, an opera house and a concert hall where the finest musical and theatre companies from the U.S.A. and abroad perform.

marily an import port with a considerable coastline trade. The waterfront contains shipbuilding and dry docks, grain elevators, oilstorage facilities and ore piers. Baltimore has historic sites but is chiefly a modern commercial and manufacturing city.

Washington, D.C., capital of the nation (756,000), has only one important industry, government. The city plan was designed by Pierre L'Enfant after the location was selected by his friend, George Washington. Radiating out from the Capitol like spokes in a wheel, the tree-lined streets of Washington cross and intertwine with many broad and beautiful avenues. Parks abound, as well as huge government buildings, mixed with museums, archives, monuments, and shrines.

In between these major cities are medium sized ones, such as Providence, Rhode Island (179,000), Hartford (158,000) and New Haven, Connecticut (137,000), Newark (382,000) and Trenton, New Jersey (104,000), and Wilmington, Delaware (80,000).

The city of Washington radiates out from the Capitol building.

Thomas Jefferson, one of the geniuses of his age, was not only a fine writer and the inventor of household aids, but an architect. He designed and built his home, Monticello, near Charlottesville in Virginia.

11

Cattle graze and birds fly over this West Virginia farm, typical of America's farm country. Agricultural colleges and government bureaus are placing great emphasis on productivity, during this period when the whole world is short of food.

Herds of cattle graze on the rich plains of Kansas before being sent to the "feedlots" for further fattening, and then to the slaughterhouse. Kansas is the leading wheat-producing state—it yields about 20 per cent of the nation's crop.

THE MIDWEST

The so-called "Heartland of America" is an extensive plain lying between the Canadian border on the north and the Ohio River and the Ozark Mountains on the south, and extending from the Appalachians on the east to the Rockies on the west. For the most part, the land is a well-watered rolling lowland. Most of the area has been subjected to glaciation with the exception of the "driftless area" of south-western Wisconsin. The Great Lakes and thousands of small lakes in the north make recreation and tourism important. The Midwest is one of the most self-sufficient areas in the entire world. Although entirely inland, it has an abundance of rail and highway systems, coupled with natural waterways. The lengthy Mississippi River (2,348 miles; 3,756 km.) flows south through the richest farming areas of the Midwest towards the Gulf of Mexico from its northern sources near Canada. The Great Lakes connect with each other and the

Capital of Minnesota, St. Paul, is seen reflected in the night waters of the Mississippi River.

man-built St. Lawrence Seaway links them to the ocean and the rest of the world.

The Central Lowlands (as the area is also called) is not just farmland, although it produces a large portion of the nation's food crops, but it also includes 28 per cent of the nation's population. The Midwest is noted for its manufacturing, its steel, car and other heavy industrial plants. Coal and iron are near, and the workers and farmers of the area form a cultural blend that makes the region the most "typically American" part of the country.

Despite the fact that there is as yet no single megalopolis to compare with that of the Northeast, a belt of cities is slowly creeping across the rich farmlands between Pittsburgh, Pennsylvania (520,000), Cleveland (750,000)

The newly erected Sears Tower in Chicago, tallest building in the world, dominates the city's skyline. Second largest city in the U.S.A., Chicago lines the shore of Lake Michigan.

Complicated cloverleaf and overpass patterns of highways are found around most cities. The idea was first exhibited at the General Motors' exhibit at the New York World's Fair of 1939–40 where it then seemed like a dream. This particular example is on the outskirts of Detroit.

A mecca for motor-conscious Americans, the Indianapolis Speedway in Indiana is the world-famous site of the annual Memorial Day 500-mile (830-km.) race.

Towering over the pine-covered Black Hills of South Dakota is Mt. Rushmore National Memorial. The 60-foot (18-m.)-high majestic faces of George Washington, Thomas Jefferson, Theodore Roosevelt and Abraham Lincoln were carved by Gutzon Borglum between 1927 and 1941.

and Toledo, Ohio (384,000), and the "Motor City," Detroit, Michigan (1,513,000). Another urbanized area reaches around the southern shore of Lake Michigan from Gary, Indiana, north to Milwaukee, and includes the second largest city in the nation, Chicago (3,370,000).

Another metropolitan area has grown up around the Twin Cities of Minneapolis (434,000) and St. Paul, Minnesota (310,000), and urban areas are growing around St. Louis (622,000) and Kansas City (502,000), both in Missouri. All the central cities have been losing population to suburbs outside the city limits.

The Great Plains west of the Prairies and Central Plains and east of the Rocky Mountains slope eastward from an elevation over 6,000 feet down to 500 feet (1,800 to 150 m.) This is an area of natural open grassland, seldom interrupted by even a man-made structure. The monotonous terrain, crisscrossed by a number of rivers, is broken by two land masses: the Badlands, an area of deep eroded valleys and sharp treeless peaks, and the Black Hills of the Dakotas which are lifted far enough above the surrounding land to receive sufficient rainfall for large spruce and pine forests. The Colorado Piedmont lowland divides the Great Plains into northern and southern portions. The northern area is dominated by the drainage of the Missouri River and its tributaries and is somewhat lower and more rolling than the southern portion. The Great Plains extend into the Southwest, where the Edwards and Stockton Plateaus of Texas form a national geographical southern boundary. Villages and a few farms are widely spaced throughout the Great Plains region.

The Bluegrass Country around Lexington is where the famous Kentucky thoroughbred horses are raised and trained.

An ocean-going ship plies the fog-covered Mississippi River near Baton Rouge, Louisiana's capital city. Many cargo vessels and tankers travel this mighty river, carrying grain, petro-chemicals and other products to the rest of the world.

THE SOUTH

The South includes the southern part of the Atlantic coastal plain and the Gulf coastal plain which extends westward along the Gulf of Mexico to the Rio Grande River that separates the U.S.A. from Mexico. Its northern extremity is the Ohio River along with the Ozark Plateau and its southernmost point is the tip of the Florida peninsula. Despite topographical differences, the South's generally subtropical climate has been a unifying factor. Economic and political bonds of the past have traditionally separated it from the rest of the nation. Today industrialism is changing the character of the region.

The coastal flats of the South are nearly 3,000 miles (4,800 km.) long. Their width varies from less than 50 to a full 500 miles (80 to 800 km.). The flood plain of the Mississippi River, which resembles the Nile Valley, becomes very wide in some places—100 miles (160 km.) across, where the soils are rich from the repeated flooding. The vast amount of sediment carried by the river extends the delta, making it almost impossible to tell where the land ends and the sea starts.

Citrus fruits come from three states, California, Florida and Texas. This is a Florida orange grove.

In central Florida is DisneyWorld, a national attraction not only for youngsters but their parents as well. It is the largest amusement park in the world, and this is Cinderella's Castle, one of the many attractions.

The Virginia and Carolina coastlines are very irregular because of the sinking coast which drowns the mouths of the rivers. The resulting tidewater bays include the Delaware and Chesapeake and Albemarle Sound. Near the shore are several great swamps including the Dismal of Virginia, the Okefenokee in Georgia and Florida, the Everglades of Florida and much of the lower Mississippi Delta in Louisiana. The Florida peninsula is made mostly of limestone. From the southern tip, keys (or tiny islands) extend 115 miles (184 km.) into the Gulf of Mexico. The coastline area of both Florida and Texas support a great citrus fruit industry, and have attracted tourist hotels and motels and

St. Louis Cathedral stands in historic Jackson Square in the heart of the French Quarter of New Orleans, Louisiana. Nearby is the Cabildo, once the seat of the Louisiana Territory government under the French and Spanish and finally the United States after the Louisiana Purchase in 1803. In the foreground is the statue of General Andrew Jackson, hero of the Battle of New Orleans.

retirement communities. Texas and Oklahoma sit on top of huge oil fields, while oil deposits have also been discovered off the shores of Louisiana.

Major cities of the South are Atlanta (497,000), Miami (335,000), New Orleans at the mouth of the Mississippi (591,000), and the biggest cities of Texas—Dallas (844,000) and Houston (1,231,000).

The interior highlands include the Ouachita Mountains and the Ozark Plateau. The southern Appalachian Mountains, including the Blue Ridge and Great Smoky Mountains, make up the other highland area. Early in the nation's history people settled into these areas and established customs that still remain.

Carlsbad Caverns in New Mexico, on the north Texas Border, the deepest cave in the U.S.A. (1,320 feet or 400 m.) has many stalactites and stalagmites and many rooms like this Dome Room.

Red Rocks, an acoustically perfect natural open-air theatre, attracts crowds for concerts on the outskirts of Denver.

THE WEST

The West is a vast area of extremes. The region runs from the Canadian border at the 49th parallel all the way to Mexico at about the 30th parallel and from the eastern Rockies 1,000 miles (1,600 km.) to the Pacific Ocean. Land heights range from Mt. Whitney, 14,494 feet (4,348 m.) to Death Valley, 282 feet (85 m.) below sea level. Rainfall in northwestern Washington exceeds 100 inches (250 cm.) annually, while Arizona receives only 2 inches (5 cm.). Montana has recorded the lowest continental temperature of −70°F. (−50°C.), and Death Valley the highest with 134°F. (52°C.). Densely populated areas adjoin unpopulated deserts and wilderness.

The Rocky Mountains, called the "Backbone of America," extend from Canada the whole way south to Mexico. Peaks and ranges of impressive grandeur separate the streams that flow west to the Pacific from those that flow east to the Atlantic. The wide rugged northern Rocky Mountains trend from northwest to southeast. The ranges are separated by long depressed trenches, the longest of which is

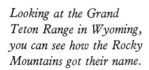

Looking at the Grand Teton Range in Wyoming, you can see how the Rocky Mountains got their name.

The Grand Canyon of the Colorado River is one of the most spectacular features of the American landscape.

the Rocky Mountain Trench (1,200 mi.; 1,920 km.). Many of the ranges like the Wind River Mountains, the Big Horns and the Grand Tetons are completely separated from the main chain. The Rockies are divided by the Wyoming Basin, which acts as an important area for transmountain travel. The southern Rockies, running almost from north to south, contain three parallel ranges. The eastern range rises to more than 14,000 feet (4,200·m.) and contains such famous mountains as Pike's Peak. Much of this area is owned by the U.S. Government and has been turned into national recreational parks and forests.

The Intermontane lies between the Rockies and the Sierra Nevada-Cascade Mountains. It includes all or parts of nine states and has a very sparse population. Diverse features include broad plateaus, buttes (isolated flat-topped, cliff-sided hills), extensive basins and many valleys. Streams eroding the area in the region of the Colorado Plateau long ago resulted in the formation of deep canyons, gorges, and badlands, the most famous of which is the Grand Canyon. Extinct volcanoes in Arizona rise to over 12,594 feet high (3,778 m.). This area is filled with buttes and mesas with sharp vertical walls. In southern California is the Imperial Valley, a region that had in its upper half extreme flooding and in its lower, very dry desert conditions. The government has solved this problem with a series of irrigation reservoirs and dams that take the over-abundance of water to the dry areas, creating a fertile valley.

Most of the people of the western states live in the valleys and coastal lowlands of California. Los Angeles, largest of the Western cities with 2,800,000 people, is the home of the motion picture industry. Between Los Angeles and San Diego to the south, in fact to the Mexican border, and north almost to San Francisco, is a string of small cities with hardly any un-

New skyscrapers in the heart of Los Angeles contrast sharply with the snow-covered slopes of the nearby mountains.

populated area in between. San Francisco (715,674) is a peninsula in itself, bordering on the famous bay of the same name. Abutting it to the north is another peninsula and between them is a narrow entrance to the Bay, called the Golden Gate. Seattle, the northernmost major Pacific city with 515,000 people, is on Puget Sound, and dominates the Pacific Northwest.

Mountains run along the coast of California, Oregon and Washington State parallel to the ocean, sometimes running almost into the sea itself. The area is subject to earthquakes.

Off to the west across the Pacific is Hawaii and to the northwest is Alaska.*

*Hawaii, Alaska and Puerto Rico are covered in separate volumes in the *Visual Geography Series*.

San Francisco's famous cable cars come up and over many of the city's steep hills. In the background is San Francisco Bay whose 450 square miles (1,100 sq. km.) constitute one of the most nearly perfect natural ports in the world.

A very popular resort city, Avalon on the island of Santa Catalina, is accessible by daily air and boat service from the mainland of southern California, 30 miles (48 km.) away. Santa Catalina, usually called Catalina, is one of the Santa Barbara (or Channel) Island group.

With the headwaters of the Yellowstone Creek in the foreground and the King's Peak rising on the right, the extremes of elevation in Utah become evident.

Mount Rainier, snow-capped all year round, can
be seen on a clear day from Seattle, 55 miles
(91 km.) away. Here it hangs like an ice-cream
cone above the clouds over the city of Olympia,
capital of the state of Washington.

The highest waterfalls in the U.S.A. and perhaps
the most spectacular in the world is Yosemite Falls,
which has a double cascade, with a total drop of
3,425 feet (1,044 m.). Yosemite National Park,
California, is visited by nearly 2,500,000 people
annually.

WATERWAYS

The U.S.A. is divided into four major drainage systems—the Atlantic, Great Lakes, Gulf Coast, and Pacific. The largest river systems are the Mississippi in the Midwest and South, the St. Lawrence in the Northeast shared with Canada, the Colorado in the West, and the Columbia in the Northwest.

The rivers of the Atlantic rise in the interior highlands and their rapid currents influence industrial development in the area. Some feed into large ocean estuaries and bays. Ocean navigation, for instance, is open on the Delaware River to Philadelphia, a distance of 40 miles (64 km.). In New England, the major rivers are the Kennebec, Merrimack, Penobscot, and Connecticut. In the Middle Atlantic states, besides the Delaware, the principal rivers are the Hudson, which empties into New York Harbor, and the Potomac. The Savannah River, which empties into a bay in Georgia, is the main river of the South Atlantic coast.

The Great Lakes drainage system enters the Atlantic Ocean in eastern Canada via the St. Lawrence River and the man-made Seaway, which in the 1950's opened the Lakes to ocean traffic. Water from the Great Lakes—Superior, Michigan, Huron, Erie, and Ontario—courses into the St. Lawrence River after cascading over Niagara Falls (between Lakes Erie and Ontario).

The Gulf drainage system, which consists almost entirely of the Mississippi and its branches, is the third largest river system in the world, exceeded only by the Amazon and the Nile. The major tributaries of the Mississippi are the Missouri, Ohio, and Arkansas. These great rivers are navigable for great distances.

The Pacific drainage system includes the Columbia and Colorado Rivers, which rise in the western mountains and flow swiftly into the Pacific Ocean or into the Gulf of California, forming waterfalls and rapids. Many of the other rivers are small and follow valleys to the ocean.

When the snows of Glacier National Park in Montana, on the Canadian border, melt in the spring, they flow into the feed waters of the Missouri River, main tributary of the Mississippi River system.

Niagara Falls is probably visited by more tourists than any other scenic spot in the U.S.A. From both the American and Canadian sides the Falls are a magnificent sight. The American Falls (shown here) are 182 feet high (56 m.), the Canadian (in the shape of a horseshoe) 176 feet (54 m.). Many industries, including aircraft, aerospace equipment, paper and chemicals, derive their power from the rushing water.

CLIMATE

The U.S.A. lies in the middle latitudes and has a characteristic climate for a large continental land mass in a zone in which circular air moves in a west-to-east direction. Southwestern California lies in a transitional zone between the westerlies and the trade winds with a characteristic semi-arid subtropical climate. Dry, hot summers and rainy, mild winters give southern California the sunny summer days ideal for the film industry and for agriculture. To the north, Oregon and Washington are subject to warm moist air that blows in from the Pacific Ocean, giving that region a wet but mild climate. Temperatures in Portland, Oregon, for example, average between 39°F. (4°C.) in January and 68°F. (20°C.) in July.

Because the Sierra Nevada-Cascade Mountain chain lies broadside to the prevailing moisture-laden westerlies, heavy rainfall falls on the windward side and semi-arid regions and deserts lie to the leeward of the mountains. From Washington and Idaho southward through the Great Basin of Nevada and Utah to New Mexico and west of the Rockies is a dry area, largely desert. East of the Rockies is a dry steppe of short grass, with extremes of temperature as great as 80°F. (38°C.). Moisture is scant and variable but, fortunately, it occurs mostly in the summer.

From the Great Plains through the Heartland, typical continental climate prevails. Westerly, circular air brings sudden weather changes, especially when cold air masses come down from Canada. Rainfall is moderate but well

A great tourist attraction, this geyser in Yellowstone National Park erupts at such regular intervals that it is called "Old Faithful."

distributed during the year. Heavy snowfall in winter and thunderstorms in summer are common. Temperatures vary widely, with as much as 100°F. (48°C.) difference between winter and summer. In general, the climate moderates toward the southern part of the area and towards the Atlantic coast.

The southeastern part of the U.S.A. has a humid subtropical climate. Rainfall is moderate to abundant, falling during all seasons of the year. The average frost-free season is more than 200 days with high summer and moderate winter temperatures. The average January temperature for New Orleans, for example, is 55°F. (13°C.)

with an average July temperature of 81°F. (27°C.). During the winter, cold waves from the North occasionally bring freezing temperatures, but protection against the cold is generally provided for the crops.

NATURAL RESOURCES

The U.S.A. was originally well endowed with minerals. In particular, it was blessed with the important minerals, coal, iron ore, and petroleum—but for producing ferroalloys, it was poorly supplied. As industrialization increased, supplies of copper, lead, zinc, iron ore and petroleum were reduced and imports became increasingly important. The mineral position of the nation is still deteriorating. The problem is accentuated by the fact that with about 6 per cent of the world's population, the U.S.A. utilizes more resources than the rest of the world put together.

Coal, a fossil fuel, is found abundantly in all parts of the U.S.A., but the eastern highlands have by far the leading amounts. Pennsylvania and West Virginia possess both bituminous (soft) and anthracite (hard) coal. Coal is highly important for steel manufacture, heating and electrical energy.

The nation was originally well supplied with petroleum, but has used it extravagantly. Although new fields are being developed offshore and in Alaska, the future supply is limited. Natural gas, which usually accompanies oil, originally plentiful, is also in short supply now. Iron ore, too, was abundant, but the supplies of the Mesabi Range in Minnesota

Mining a seam of anthracite coal in the Pennsylvania fields is a hazardous occupation, but the country is becoming more dependent on coal for its fuel.

Sequoia National Park in California is named for these giant conifers, among the world's tallest, as high as 350 feet (105 m.), and oldest—some specimens are believed to be over 3,000 years old.

have been depleted, and imports from Canada and South America are increasing. The important metals used in ferroalloys (special steels)—manganese, chromium, titanium, tungsten, and vanadium—are in such short supply that they must be imported.

The nation is rich in agricultural resources. Western New York State, the Nashville Basin, the Midwest, the Sacramento Valley, and the Willamette Valley of Oregon, are among the richest agricultural areas in the world. The Midwest with its agricultural products of corn, wheat, soybeans, cattle, and hogs is one of the largest, richest farmlands in the world.

FLORA AND FAUNA

Originally, the natural vegetation of the U.S.A. consisted roughly of half woodland, one-third grassland and one-sixth desert. Early Americans destroyed much of the woodlands, but today a tremendous conservation campaign is helping to rebuild them. The northern forests, which run from the Atlantic to the

The giant saguaro cactus, which grows to the height of a tree, is a familiar sight in the dry regions of the Southwest.

Mississippi and from Canada down the Appalachians, are mixed coniferous and deciduous. Typical mammals inhabiting these forests are beavers, moose, hares, bears,

Yuccas are plants of the lily family found in the southwestern states and also in Florida. Early Spanish colonists in Florida planted yuccas around their settlements as a defense, since the stiff, sharp, swordlike leaves of these plants form an almost impenetrable barrier.

Santa Cruz, California, are the tallest trees in the world, many attaining a height of over 350 feet (105 m.). In the Rockies, a few large mammals survive, in greatly reduced numbers. These include bears, bighorn sheep, wolves, Rocky Mountain goats, and the American elk.

The woodlands in the Middle Atlantic states contain a greater variety of trees than any other area. Oak, hickory, maple, beech, ash, tulip, and dogwood make up the bulk of the forests. Further to the south, magnolia, laurel, rhododendron, and pine are predominant, and on the Atlantic and Gulf coasts, palms and palmettos occur from the Carolinas south. The beaver, black bear, deer, opossum, rabbit, fox, otter, and raccoon, as well as ruffed grouse, cardinals and some wild turkeys (to name a few of the many birds) flourish in the central and southern woods. Shrimp and shellfish abound in the Gulf of Mexico and around the Florida peninsula, as do alligators in the swamps and rivers of this region.

Canadian lynxes, wolverines, deer, foxes, red squirrels, and martens. Brook and lake trout, bass, muskelunge, and whitefish are native to the cool lakes, while loons, wild geese and ducks feed and nest in the area. Lobsters inhabit the waters of the Atlantic from Maine to Massachusetts. Cod is abundant in the area too.

No large deciduous forests exist west of the Great Plains. Forests in this region are composed of pine, fir, western hemlock, and cedar. The redwoods and sequoias, which extend in a belt from southwestern Oregon as far south as

Because of the excellent soil and climate, very little tall prairie grass remains in the Plains states. It has been replaced by farm crops, as have the vast herds of bison that once grazed on these lands.

The American bison or buffalo was on the verge of extinction before the last herds were put on a reservation in a national park and encouraged to reproduce.

Although many other animals in the U.S.A. are in danger of extinction, most deer species are not. In the Eastern states especially, deer have increased in recent years, as more and more farmland, once cleared for cultivation, has been returned to woodland. The reasons for this are that deer are woodland animals and that the small farms of the Northeast can no longer compete with the large ones of the Midwest. Deer often invade suburban gardens in New York State and New England.

In the deserts of the West are found sagebrush, yuccas, cactus, and Joshua trees. The deserts are not without animal life, and occasionally, jack rabbits (very long-eared hares), pronghorns, coyotes, armadillos, kangaroo rats, pumas, iguanas, horned toads, and Gila monsters can be seen. Fishing off the Pacific coast for various species of crabs, abalones and other shellfish once found in large numbers is now restricted by law.

Throughout much of the U.S.A., especially in the East, some of the most common weeds and wildflowers are immigrants from Europe—brought by the first settlers and gone wild. Two of the most commonly seen birds—the starling and the English sparrow—were likewise introduced from Europe.

Black bears roam freely in Yellowstone Park, oldest and largest of U.S. National Parks.

Cliff dwellings, perched on mesas or on the ledges of canyon walls in the Southwest, were built by the ancestors of the Pueblo Indians as defense against nomadic tribes. These well-preserved ruins called the Cliff Palace, dating back to the 12th century, are in Mesa Verde National Park in southwestern Colorado. Others like it are in New Mexico, Arizona and Utah.

2. HISTORY

WHEN IN THE EARLY MORNING of October 12, 1492, sailors on the ships of Columbus sighted one of the islands in the Caribbean Sea, a new, exciting era began—the exploration and colonization of the New World by Europe. (Columbus never set foot on the mainland of North America.) Columbus' discovery was not an accident but the result of many changes taking place in Europe and primarily the result of a need for new trade routes to the East. When it was realized that a new world had been discovered, Spanish, French and English explorers began to search for gold and silver and a passage to India, China and the East. They encountered the first inhabitants of America, the Indians, who probably arrived many thousands of years ago over a land bridge from Asia into Alaska. The hundreds of native tribes of what is now the United States could roughly be divided into the Indians of the eastern woodlands, hunters of the plains, village dwellers of the Southwest, seed-gatherers of the Intermontane, and fishermen of the Northwest.

EXPLORATION

The Spanish were the first explorers of the territory that is now the United States. Ponce de

Léon, searching for gold and silver and a Fountain of Youth, began exploring Florida in 1513. Other Spaniards attempted to establish themselves in Virginia and Florida, but were repulsed by hostile Indians. Hernando de Soto, in 1539, was more successful although he did not find the gold he was searching for. He explored much of the southeastern United States including the Mississippi River. In 1540, Francisco Coronado marched from Mexico into Arizona, across the plains into Kansas, and finally into Colorado. Although none of the Spanish explorers found gold, they added immense territory to the Spanish Empire—all of the southeastern and western portion of the United States. Just as important was the spread of the Spanish language, religion, and culture into North America.

The English and French had their chance to explore the New World. The English in 1497 and 1498 sent John Cabot to the North American coast where he sailed from Labrador to the Carolinas. The French explored the St. Lawrence River and the Gulf region. Giovanni da Verrazano, in 1524, sailed along the coast from North Carolina to Nova Scotia, discovering New York Harbor, and ten years later Jacques Cartier discovered the Gulf of St. Lawrence. Under Samuel de Champlain's leadership in 1608, a French colony was established at Quebec, and exploration was pushed to Lakes Champlain and Ontario. French missionaries, in the following years, pushed westward through the Great Lakes to the Mississippi and finally down the great river to its mouth. Louis Joliet and Father Jacques Marquette participated in exploration, but it was Robert Cavalier de la Salle who first reached the mouth of the

Jamestown has been reconstructed as it was in 1607, complete with church, storehouse, guardhouse and houses—there are even guards dressed in the style of the early 1600's.

Mayflower II at Plymouth, Massachusetts, is a full-scale reproduction of the type of ship that brought the Pilgrims to America in 1620. It is berthed at State Pier in Plymouth near Plymouth Rock, where the Pilgrims landed to found the first permanent settlement north of Virginia.

COLONIZATION

Although the Spanish failed in several attempts at colonization, in 1565 they settled St. Augustine in Florida, which today is the oldest surviving European settlement in the U.S.A. The French were interested primarily in the fur trade with Indians and did not attempt much colonization. The British began to establish permanent colonies beginning in 1607, when Jamestown was founded on the Virginia coast. It was followed by Plymouth Plantation in Massachusetts in 1620. The most successful early colony was the Massachusetts Bay Colony, established in 1630 around the Boston area. Waves of Puritan settlers followed as the colony grew along the coast and into the interior. Two other New England colonies—Rhode Island and Connecticut—were established by emigrants dissatisfied with the Puritans in Massachusetts, and a third, New Hampshire, was chartered in 1679.

Mississippi. As a result of the French exploration, the French claimed territory along the St. Lawrence River, the Great Lakes, and the interior of North America.

Not until the reign of Queen Elizabeth did the English seek to reclaim the discoveries of John Cabot. Sir Walter Raleigh, in the 1580's, attempted but failed to establish colonies along the coast of North Carolina.

A familiar painting shows Pilgrims of the Massachusetts Bay colony on their way to church on Sunday, some of them armed in the event of an Indian attack.

William Penn (standing, arms outstretched) was a Colonial leader who tried to treat the Indians fairly. In establishing the colony of Pennsylvania he negotiated honestly with the Delaware tribe and lived up to his agreements with them.

English colonies in New York, New Jersey, Delaware, Maryland, and Pennsylvania were founded between 1624 and 1682. New York had originally been settled by the Dutch, but it was captured by the English without a battle in 1664. Delaware, originally settled by Swedes, was taken over by the Dutch, and finally became an English colony. Pennsylvania, the most democratic colony, called "the holy experiment," was founded by a Quaker, William Penn, in 1682.

The southern colonies expanded from Virginia when settlers moved southward between 1653 and 1660. South Carolina, founded in 1670 at Charleston, became a refuge for French Huguenots. The last of the original 13 colonies was founded in 1733, when James Oglethorpe established Georgia.

By 1753, over 750,000 people had crossed the ocean to the new land, and most of them had found homes along the Atlantic seaboard. Although the English predominated, there were large numbers of French, Welsh, Swiss, Danes, Scotch-Irish, Germans, and Dutch. By the beginning of the Revolutionary War, the population was over 2,500,000. Europeans were not the only inhabitants, however; about 400,000 black slaves had been brought over from Africa to work in the fields and homes of the Southern colonists.

Already the frontier was shifting westward across the Allegheny Mountains, and it was only a matter of time before England and France clashed again over supremacy in North America. The French and Indian War (1754–63) culminated a series of four wars fought between England and France. England won the wars with the aid of colonial militia, and at the Peace of Paris, France ceded all of Canada, Florida (Spain had been France's ally) and the territory east of the Mississippi except New Orleans, which was given to Spain.

REVOLUTIONARY WAR PERIOD

The estrangement between England and the colonies started when new English policies were put into effect after the war. The previous period might be described as one of benign neglect of the colonies by England, but England's war debt was huge, and the King and Parliament expected the colonies to pay a share of it. Laws requiring the colonists to trade only with England and to pay taxes on goods purchased were strictly enforced. The colonists resisted by smuggling. Britain then stationed troops in America, and the colonists were expected to pay for their upkeep. The colonists protested that they should not be taxed this way without representation. England closed the port of Boston and suspended the Massachusetts legislature because of the "Boston Tea Party," an affair in which a shipload of tea was dumped into the water by patriots disguised as Indians. Many of the colonists now began to talk about rebellion.

Fighting began on April 19, 1775, when 800 British troops left Boston for nearby Lexington and Concord to capture supplies of the colonists' ammunition. When the British arrived at Lexington, they found a band of 76 Minutemen drawn up across the village green. In the confusion a shot was fired, and the war began. The

To protest British restrictions on the importing of tea, citizens of Boston dressed as Indians, boarded British ships in Boston Harbor and dumped their cargo into the water. This action was known as the "Boston Tea Party."

The British under General Cornwallis, after being surrounded by American and French troops in 1781, surrendered to General Washington, marking the end of the Revolutionary War.

following June, the colonists laid siege to Boston, and although defeated at the Battle of Bunker Hill, they continued the fight with renewed energy.

A Continental Congress, made up of representatives from all the 13 colonies, assumed the government and directed the Continental Army with George Washington as commander-in-chief. On July 4, 1776, in Philadelphia, the Congress signed a Declaration of Independence. At first, the war went badly for the ill-supplied Continental Army, reaching a low point in 1777–78, when the depleted Continentals wintered at Valley Forge, Pennsylvania. Here, however, they were pulled together by George Washington with the aid of two foreign officers—the Frenchman Lafayette and the German Baron von Steuben. The American victory at Saratoga brought the French into the war on the side of the Americans. The end of the fighting occurred when the British were defeated on the peninsula at Yorktown, Vir-

ginia, in 1781, by a combination of land troops and ships. In the treaty that followed, Great Britain recognized the independence of the United States and set the Mississippi River as its western boundary.

During the Revolutionary War, the Continental Congress had drawn up Articles of Confederation to provide for a loose confederation of states with a weak central government. It turned out that, under this system, Congress could not enforce its actions, levy or collect taxes, or control commerce. Government debts were unpaid, the Continental dollar deteriorated, and the states ignored Congress. In 1787, a convention was called to strengthen the central government.

Fifty-five delegates from the states gathered in Independence Hall in Philadelphia to write a new constitution. This group was one of the most remarkable assemblages of democratic thinkers ever gathered at one place. Almost all the colonial leaders were there—including

Federal Hall in New York City stands on the spot at Nassau and Wall Streets where George Washington took the oath of office as first President of the U.S.A. in 1789.

George Washington, James Madison, Thomas Jefferson, Benjamin Franklin, Robert Morris, and Alexander Hamilton.

The convention became a series of struggles and compromises, but the Constitution which resulted from their work lives on today as an inspiration to all the democracies of the world, and the laws made under it became the supreme law of the whole country. Ratification by 9 states was soon accomplished, and the new Constitution went into effect in 1789. The first 10 amendments, called the Bill of Rights, were added immediately after.

EARLY NATIONAL PERIOD

The first president, George Washington, faced the serious problems of leading a new nation, securing a firm financial footing, and formulating a neutral foreign policy. Some of

the perplexing problems with Great Britain regarding the western frontier line, trade, and debts were cleared up by the Jay Treaty. In establishing new policies, opposition hardened, and political parties developed. The election of

Here, Betsy Ross stitched the first American flag in 1776. The flag with its circle of stars, one for each of the 13 original states, was officially adopted by Congress in 1777. The Ross home in Philadelphia, not far from Independence Hall, is a tourist shrine.

36

The Hermitage near Nashville, Tennessee, home of Andrew Jackson, seventh President of the United States, is a typical Southern mansion of the early 19th century. The tall graceful columns and fine doorway reflect the elegance of life in the South, especially before the Civil War. The furniture and gardens of this large estate are preserved just as they were in Jackson's day.

Thomas Jefferson in 1800 saw for the first time political party pitted against political party.

As settlers occupied the lands west of the Allegheny Mountains, new states were admitted to the union. Indian resistance to encroachment on their land led to a series of battles, after which the Indians were forced to cede land to the U.S.A. for small sums of money. In 1803, the size of the nation doubled with the purchase of the vast 887,000 sq. mi. (2,156,700 sq. km.) Louisiana Territory from Napoleon, who needed money to continue his wars for France. The national territory expanded again in 1819, when Florida was purchased. Thus by 1820, the U.S.A. extended from Canada to the Gulf of Mexico and from the Atlantic to the Rocky Mountains.

The War of 1812 with Great Britain was fought because American sailors were being seized and trouble occurred on the frontiers with Canada. Many Westerners looked at Canada as the next area to be annexed. News travelled slowly in those days, and the final battle, fought after the Treaty of Ghent was signed, was won at New Orleans by the Americans and provided a hero and future president, Andrew Jackson.

The U.S.A. asserted itself in foreign affairs with the issuance of the Monroe Doctrine in 1823, which stated that the American hemisphere was no longer to be considered as subject to future colonization by any European power. The Doctrine, a reaction against Spain's attempt to regain its colonies in North and South America, which had become republics like the U.S.A., had the support of Great Britain, and other European nations did not attempt to violate it.

Economic and cultural differences between

Cumberland Gap was the gateway to the Kentucky wilderness for pioneers such as Daniel Boone, and later for settlers on the way to Kentucky and further west. Because of its location, high in the mountains connecting Virginia, Tennessee and Kentucky, it was a strategic point during the War between the States, also.

the North (including the Midwest) and South began to develop early, and, as the nation expanded, the differences became severe. The South remained agrarian, depending upon the commercial crops of cotton and tobacco with plenty of slaves to work the fields. In the North, manufacturing of textiles, iron, and glass was increasingly important. In the fertile Midwest,

independent, free farmers became dominant. Neither the factory workers nor the farmers wanted to compete with slave manpower.

In the meantime, pioneers continued to open up the western lands. Daniel Boone (1734–1820) led the settlement of the lands just west of the Appalachian Mountains. Meriwether Lewis and William Clark led an expedition (1803–06)

The Lewis and Clark expedition built flatboats to carry them down the Snake River—such boats were widely used at that time on the Mississippi, as shown here.

The Alamo in San Antonio was the scene of a heroic but futile defense by a handful of Texans in 1836.

up the Missouri River and across the Rockies to the Pacific. David (Davy) Crockett (1786–1836) was one of numerous Americans who settled in Texas (then claimed by Mexico) and who perished at the Alamo in the Texas Revolution. The Texans defeated the Mexican forces shortly after and declared an independent republic which lasted until 1845, when Texas joined the United States.

The discovery of gold in California in 1848 spurred migration across the continent, and trains of covered wagons headed west, facing drought, famine and fierce resistance by the proud Indians of the Plains tribes. Most of these settlers headed for California, but some remained along the way, in isolated trading posts, forts, and way stations.

As new states were admitted into the Union, a

The Gold Rush—the scramble of the "Forty-Niners" across the continent in 1849—was set off by the discovery of gold at Sutter's Mill in California in 1848.

As a wagon train pushed westwards across the plains, scouts from the train would climb hills or buttes to scan the horizon for possible danger.

balance between slave and non-slave states was attempted. By the time Texas joined the Union in 1845, the Oregon Territory border conflict became settled by treaty with Great Britain in 1846, and the southwest, including California, was secured from Mexico after the Mexican War in 1848, the nation stretched from ocean to ocean. Now the questions of free state or slave state, the rights of the states, and balance of power between North and South came to a head. When Abraham Lincoln was elected President in 1860 as the candidate of the northern Republican Party, the southern states seceded from the Union.

WAR AND RECONSTRUCTION

Four years (1861–65) of terrible war between the states followed. The 23 states of the North had the advantages of industry, money, and population (23,000,000 against 5,000,000) while the 11 states of the South initially had the more

able generals. The Northern grand strategy was to cut the South in two and shut off all supplies

An early method of transportation on the Mississippi and other rivers was the side-wheeler. The paddle-wheeler shown above is representative of the type of ship that plied the Mississippi between Louisville, Kentucky, and New Orleans in the mid-19th century. A few such boats are still used as tourist attractions.

As a young man, Abraham Lincoln earned money by poling a raft and working on a ferry on the Ohio River.

In the South, before the Civil War, blacks were bought and sold in slave markets such as this—as though they were livestock. By the end of the war, President Lincoln had proclaimed freedom for all slaves. It took another 100 years before the blacks obtained all their civil rights.

The many statues on the battlefield at Gettysburg, Pennsylvania, commemorate the most furious battle ever fought on American soil. The Federal Army with 97,000 men withstood the invasion of the Confederate Army with about 75,000 men under General Robert E. Lee. After three days of furious fighting the Confederates withdrew. It was on this battlefield that Lincoln delivered his most famous address. This statue is of General Lee.

The Lincoln Memorial, one of the many shrines of Washington, D.C., is separated from the Washington Monument by two long reflecting pools. The colossal seated statue of Lincoln is by Daniel Chester French, and on the walls are carved Lincoln's famous Gettysburg Address and his Second Inaugural Address.

Before railways were built, and even long after, stagecoaches were a chief means of transport.

and materials by blockading ports and by controlling the Mississippi River. In the beginning, the war went badly for the North with military defeat after defeat. The farthest north the South marched was into Pennsylvania in 1862, but after the defeat at Gettysburg, it was only a matter of time for the Southern armies to be crushed by the superior numbers of the North.

During the years immediately after the War, the nation was slowly reunited by policies established in the North. Three amendments were added to the Constitution which freed the slaves, recognized blacks as citizens, and gave them the right to vote and hold office. The amendments did not get enforced completely, however, and the treatment of racial minorities continued to be a problem for more than 100 years. The South had been devastated by the War and remained an economically poor section until the mid-20th century, when progress began to be made in improving methods of farming and building new industries.

WESTWARD MOVEMENT

Following the War, the expanses of the West started to be settled, until, about 1890, the frontier days came to an end. Except for portions of the west coast and the southwest, and Utah (which was settled in 1847, by the

Following the Civil War, Wichita, Kansas, became the chief point for shipping cattle east by rail.

In 1844, Brigham Young, a stern man, led the Mormons in a trek across the U.S.A. to their new "promised land." They were the first large transcontinental group to migrate and establish a permanent settlement, which they did at Salt Lake City, Utah.

Mormons, a sect fleeing religious persecution), the area had been inhabited by Indians who resisted the taking of their lands by fighting.

This was the era of the Wild West. The Plains Indians, who had developed a unique culture in a relatively short time, were typified by the Sioux. The lives of these people had been greatly altered by the introduction of the horse about 1700, from the Spanish-held lands to the south. Whereas once they had stalked the

Expansion of transcontinental railways began in 1864 when the Central Pacific was pushed east from California to meet the Union Pacific; by 1869 the first transcontinental road was complete. Often the workmen lived on construction trains like this which moved along as the rails were laid. Supplies were carried by wagons like those on the left. Indian attacks were frequent and not all construction workers were protected by soldiers with friendly Indian scouts like the group above.

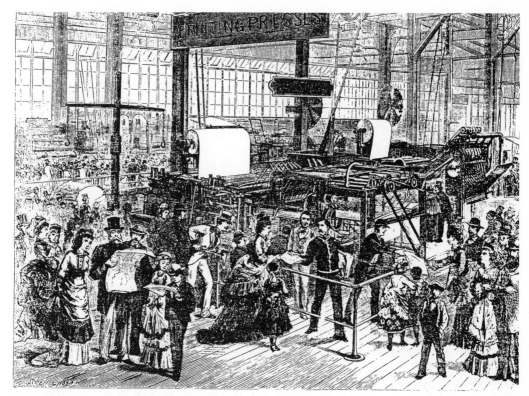

In the 1870's, new rotary presses came into use, transforming the newspaper and publishing industries, and thus helping greatly to build the power of the press as a major factor in U.S. life.

American bison, popularly called buffalo, on foot, they now did it on horseback. The horse also increased their range and effectiveness in making war on each other and later in attacking the wagon trains of the settlers and the outposts of the U.S. Cavalry. They resisted the settlers valiantly, but one by one they were defeated—the Sioux, the Cheyenne, the Arapaho, the Crow, the Pawnee, the Comanche, the Blackfoot, the Kiowa and the Apache. A factor that contributed greatly to their defeat was the wholesale destruction by the whites of the vast bison herds, their chief source of food.

Ranchers, miners, and farmers quickly moved into the area. A transcontinental railroad was built across the West with the aid of the national government. The Homestead Act of 1862 provided free land to people who wanted to farm. A 20-year period of open range, long cattle drives, cowboys, and cow towns followed. Miners flocked to the mountains in search of gold and silver. Farmers, by using new methods of dry farming and irrigation, expanded into the area.

GROWTH OF CITIES

With a great wave of industrialization, new cities developed and old ones grew, so that today more Americans live in cities than in rural areas. To the established cities of the country, Boston, New York and Philadelphia, new, large cities in the Midwest and West were added. Cleveland, Pittsburgh, Detroit, Dallas, Houston, San Francisco, and Los Angeles were but some of the largest. Chicago, because of its central location on a Great Lake, grew to dominate the industry and transportation of the middle of the continent. Political power slowly shifted about the beginning of the 20th century from the rural areas to the cities, as workers formed unions and became politically conscious. Rural workers who left their farms to work in the cities, and millions of immigrants joined the ranks of the workers. The flood

45

The Exposition of 1893 at Chicago, Illinois, marked the 400th anniversary of the discovery of America by Christopher Columbus. Many of the 150 buildings of varied architectural styles were designed by noted architects of the day, including Richard Morris Hunt, Louis Sullivan, who did the Transportation Building, and Charles F. McKim, who built the Agricultural Palace. The large classical building across the lagoon in the picture had the interesting name "The Hall of Manufactures and Liberal Arts" and was the biggest of all the structures.

continued until immigration laws were passed to slow the stream.

As the economy grew, a new force, "Big Business," appeared. Businessmen had helped greatly in the building of America, but in the late 19th century some became too powerful, and sometimes by unscrupulous means. The latter, called "Robber Barons," made fortunes in railways, mining and finance at the expense of the American people. Others sought to monopolize their own industry through the creation of trusts. President Theodore Roosevelt, during two terms of office (1901–09), fought the monopolies and laws were passed and

President Theodore Roosevelt, later famous for his effort to curb "Big Business," led a regiment called the "Rough Riders," in the Spanish-American War.

The 1920's was a period of great activity and prosperity in the U.S.A.— at least until the stock market crash of 1929.

government agencies created to control them, at his instigation.

THE U.S.A. AS A WORLD POWER

By the end of the 19th century, the U.S.A. had filled out from coast to coast, and now it turned to foreign trade and affairs and acquisition of territories overseas. Hawaii was annexed in 1898. A minor war, the Spanish-American, which ended in victory in 1898, added Puerto Rico and the Philippine Islands as territories, and announced to the world that the U.S.A. was a naval power to be reckoned with. With two coasts and possessions in both oceans, the difficulty of maintaining a two-ocean navy became evident. A way of getting ships from Atlantic to Pacific was needed, and the U.S.A.

sponsored the construction of the Panama Canal, which was completed in 1914. The nation grew faster and faster. Because it had so many resources, had so much world trade, and because it sympathized with the Allies against Germany, it was drawn into World War I. At its conclusion, President Woodrow Wilson proposed a League of Nations, but the U.S. Senate refused to confirm America's joining. However, the U.S.A. could not turn back from its position as a world power.

20TH-CENTURY AMERICA

After World War I, the desire to return to "normalcy" resulted in an era called the "Roaring Twenties," with new prosperity, prohibition against drinking alcohol (a law that was

Franklin Delano Roosevelt was the only President to serve three terms and part of a fourth. The picture shows him reviewing the United States fleet as Commander-in-Chief of the armed forces during World War II.

President John Kennedy (right) is seen in 1960 during his presidential campaign with his brother Senator Robert Kennedy, and Vice-President (later President) Lyndon Johnson.

hardly obeyed), and the sale of a cheap Model T Ford car. But this era was brought to a sudden halt with the economic crash of 1929. In answer to the people's despair during the worldwide depression of the 1930's that had been set off by the U.S. stock market crash, President Franklin D. Roosevelt turned the tide with a New Deal, consisting of public works projects, relief for the jobless and reform of the economy, with many new laws and governmental agencies. The New Deal was not completely successful in ending the Depression but, by 1939, Europe got involved in World War II, and the U.S.A. became the largest supplier of Britain and the Allies.

America entered the War after the Japanese attacked Pearl Harbor on December 7, 1941. After succeeding in the struggle against Germany and Italy, the military might of the U.S.A. was turned against Japan. The world's most horrible war ended with the dropping of the atomic bomb on two cities in Japan, and the world entered the atomic age.

The post-war years have focused on the problem of world peace. The U.S.A. provided leadership for the free world in setting up the United Nations Organization, and in conducting the "Cold War" of the 1950's against the Soviet Union and the other communist nations. Through the Marshall Plan, which provided economic aid to Europe, and the NATO Treaty, the U.S.A. tried to confine communism to limited areas. The Korean and Vietnam Wars were the culmination of that effort. More recently, the U.S.A. has begun a policy of summit meetings and détente with the Soviet Union and the Peoples Republic of China. As more nations acquire the atomic bomb, the need to stop the risk of worldwide war is recognized by the major powers. The U.N. has shown weaknesses, and has become merely an international forum. The U.S.A. is taking a leadership rôle in arbitrating problems in the Middle East, and continues to trade with almost all countries.

Although the Soviet Union was the first country to put a man in space, the United States turned its resources more effectively toward the conquest of space, and in 1969, was first to put a man on the moon.

Not only was a man rocketed to the moon under the U.S.A.'s national space administration, but a vehicle was driven around the mountains and craters, and pictures were sent back to earth for TV viewing.

Sitting on the steps of the Supreme Court Building in Washington, D.C., under the engraved lettering proclaiming "Equal Justice for All," a group of blacks from Arkansas protested in 1958 against unfair segregation in the high school in Little Rock.

3. GOVERNMENT

THE FOUNDATIONS of American government are based on two documents, the Declaration of Independence and the Constitution. The Declaration of Independence defiantly stated in 1776 that governments are instituted among men by the consent of the governed. The Constitution outlines how that principle is to be incorporated into the traditions of 13 separate states. It states that the national government makes the supreme law of the land. It further describes the relationship among the governments, national and state, the powers of each, and the structure of the national government. Still the document is broad and flexible enough to be a living document, responsive to the needs of each generation.

THE FEDERAL GOVERNMENT

The national government is delegated powers by the Constitution which include the levying of taxes, regulating foreign trade and the coining of money, and declaring war. All other powers are reserved to the states. The federal government is composed of three branches; the legislative, the executive, and the judicial. The legislative branch or Congress is composed of two separate houses. Membership in the House of Representatives is based on population with a present limit of 436, proportioned according to population. The Senate's membership is 100, two from each of the 50 states. Bills may originate from either body, except for

President John F. Kennedy addresses a joint session of Congress to deliver a "State of the Union" message.

revenue bills, which must begin in the House of Representatives. To become law, a bill must pass both houses and be signed by the President. Representatives are elected every 2 years, and Senators every 6 years, one third of them every 2 years.

The President is elected every 4 years and has the responsibility to administer the laws of the land, conduct foreign affairs, and make recommendations to Congress. He may veto acts passed by Congress, but his veto can be overridden by a two-thirds majority in each house. Because of the complexity of modern problems, the Presidency has gained power through the years.

The judicial branch is composed of a Supreme Court and lower courts established by Congress. The Supreme Court, although not granted the power in the Constitution, has assumed the power of judicial review, and the right to declare a law unconstitutional. The powers and limitations of each branch are designed to provide for a system of checks and balances among the branches of government.

STATE GOVERNMENTS

The idea of a central government and state governments existing under a federal system was new when it began in the U.S.A. As time passed, the wording of the "elastic clause" by which powers not assumed by the Federal government remained with the states, was stretched by the government in Washington to cover many actions, eroding the power of the states. The superior taxing ability of the national government has also eroded state power.

Most of the state governments are patterned after the national government. Legislatures, for the most part, are composed of two houses, governors head an executive branch, and the judicial system is lodged in a supreme court and lower courts. Political units in each state are the creations of the state government, and a confusing array of local governments exist in most states. More than 100,000 city, county, town, township, and miscellaneous district governments exist to the confusion of many people. But it is at the local level that most citizens learn to participate in government, and the local units are considered by many to be the foundation of democracy.

CIVIL RIGHTS

The most perplexing domestic problem still remaining is civil rights. Basic to the Constitution and its amendments is the protection of the individual from actions of governments and others. Due process of law and equal protection of each individual are the cornerstones of civil rights. Recent Supreme Court decisions have carefully prescribed the treatment of arrested persons as a part of due process. Critics, on the other hand, claim that the police power is so circumscribed that law and order are difficult, if not impossible, to maintain.

Historically Blacks, Spanish-speaking Americans, and the American Indians have been treated as second-class citizens, denied equal treatment under the law. The Supreme Court in 1954 with its "Brown vs. Topeka" decision started a breakthrough when it declared that the theory of "separate but equal" is inherently unequal. Progress has continued, after civil rights protest actions and with the passage of the Civil Rights Act of 1965. Focusing on equal education, housing, and employment, this progress has been remarkable, considering the slowness of previous reforms to be effected. No one, however, believes that the ideal has yet been attained.

ARMED FORCES

The U.S. Armed Forces, a highly respected institution until called into question after the Korean War, and especially during the Vietnam campaign, consist of the Army, Navy, Air Force and two smaller services, the Marines, attached to the Navy, and the Coast Guard, which functions under the Navy in time of war and in peace time, under the U.S. Department of Transportation.

The need for strong defense, dating from the uncertain days of the young Republic, is widely recognized by U.S. citizens. However, today an increasing demand exists for closer scrutiny of U.S. defense expenditures and of the influence of the "military establishment."

BUREAUCRACY

The U.S. taxpayer sometimes expresses disbelief at the number of government agencies which his taxes support. At the federal level alone, there exists a somewhat confusing assortment of offices grouped under the President, as extensions of the executive power in specialized areas.

Besides the Cabinet, which consists of 11 Departments (Ministries), each headed by a Secretary reporting to the President, there are about 2 dozen independent agencies reporting directly to the President. Since these agencies are often concerned in activities under the jurisdiction of the Departments, there is re-duplication of effort, inter-agency rivalry and, consequently, additions to the cost of government, which many critics consider unnecessary.

In addition, in Washington, there is a kind of "shadow" government—the lobbies. The lobbies, so called because their members originally used to wait in the lobbies of Congress in order to gain the attention of legislators and press their point of view upon them, are the representatives of special-interest groups with offices in Washington. They represent a broad range of U.S. life—industry, finance, agriculture, political and social movements, trade unions, regional and religious groups, professional associations, down to American Indians

An Army Engineers group practices crossing a lake to hold a beachhead.

Low-cost housing on a large scale came into being under President Franklin Roosevelt, and has continued ever since, although many people in the U.S.A. are still ill-housed, especially members of minority races who have moved into the northern and western states, where, until World War II, they were very few in number.

and Eskimos (from Alaska). Their purpose is to present their point of view, in an organized manner, to the lawmakers of the nation and to various executive agencies. Some of the more powerful lobbies, however, have been charged with exerting undue influence, even though they have no official status.

THE POWER OF THE PRESS

One of the guarantees provided by the drafters of the U.S. Constitution is freedom of the press. A powerful network of news media—press, television, and radio—stretches across the U.S.A., scrutinizing the actions of government at all levels. The "watchdog" function of the U.S. free press has often served the interest of the American people in exposing unethical or illegal situations in government—an outstanding case in point being the Watergate scandal of 1973-74.

POLITICAL PARTIES

Almost since the founding of the nation, the two-party system has been the basis of political activity. The two major parties, the Democrats and the Republicans, traditionally dominate the political arena, although nothing in the Constitution states that there can be only two major parties. To some foreign observers, the difference between these parties is not clear. Actually, the Republican Party receives support from financiers, industrialists, farmers and people of small towns of the North and West, while the Democrats attract trade unionists, minorities and people of the large cities, and have been traditionally the party of the 11 Southern States that seceded. Both parties are really coalitions, with conservative and liberal wings. There are numerous minor parties in the U.S.A. but none of these is important in federal politics.

Around Detroit, Michigan, the big car manufacturers are located. Here a motor is being installed into a body in assembly line operations. Henry Ford revolutionized the industry in the early 1900's with three concepts—the production line, catering to a low-priced mass market, and a $5.00 a day wage, which was twice the going rate!

4. THE ECONOMY

THE AMERICAN ECONOMY developed into the richest in the world as a result of isolation, ample natural resources, cheap manpower supply, available money, and inventiveness. Historically, the U.S.A. has not had powerful neighbors to divert its attention from the development of its resources. Cheap manpower was made available through the importation of slaves before 1865 and millions of immigrants from Europe. The utilization of standardized parts and the mass production assembly line, skilfully managed, and combined with the nation's resources, resulted in high productivity.

Big business and its ability to mobilize capital and matériel for mass production is interrelated with several other institutions which have been developed more fully in the U.S.A. than in any other large nation, and which figure importantly in the American economy.

One of these is the development of the stock market on a nationwide basis, with large numbers of working, professional and middle-class people owning shares in American corporations. Another is the development of American trade unions into powerful bastions of "vested interest," with enormous reserves of capital to be used not only for the benefit of members, but for investment. A third is the growth of huge private foundations, such as the Ford and Rockefeller Foundations, and the Carnegie Corporation, which make grants to science, medicine, the arts, education and other fields.

American business early recognized that mass production could only work if a mass market existed. To create such a market, industry called upon advertising to spread knowledge of its products and create a demand. Advertising in turn depended upon a highly developed communications system—press, radio, television, and postal service. Next, an efficient distribu-

(Above) When a large car manufacturer closed its plants in Milwaukee and Kenosha, Wisconsin, it threw 3,000 employees out of work. They lined up next day applying for new jobs or unemployment insurance. Union funds are used for strike periods and after insurance payments are used up.

(Left) Modern shopping centers like this one in Schaumberg, Illinois, draw customers from city and suburbs, offering vast quantities of nationally advertised products. This center includes 4 department stores and 200 other shops. Many acres of parking lots are provided.

A merchandising pioneer, F. W. Woolworth, opened the first "5 and 10 cents" store in the 1870's. The chain of Woolworth stores was the first to bring a great variety of low-priced items to factory and farm workers.

Benjamin Franklin (1706–90) was an inventor, a noted statesman, philosopher and scientist, a true versatile "Renaissance" man. He had only two years of schooling, but never stopped educating himself. Among his many inventions were the lightning rod, bifocal spectacles and the Franklin stove. Here he is showing that lightning and electricity are the same thing by flying a kite with a key at the end of the string into a rain cloud.

tion network was required to service the market —improved transportation and warehousing and the centralization of consumer outlets in department stores, supermarkets and shopping "centers." Lastly, a universal system of ready credit was evolved, not only for businesses but for individual consumers.

All of these techniques and systems were developed and put into practice in the U.S.A., long before they were adopted by other nations.

INVENTIONS

Benjamin Franklin, who drew electricity from the clouds, was America's first scientific inventor. Thomas Jefferson invented numerous devices, and Thomas Edison with a multitude of inventions, including the phonograph, was certainly the most famous.

The U.S.A.'s economic advance has been greatly forwarded by the practical inventiveness

Alexander Graham Bell, in 1877, first demonstrated his invention, the telephone. Today, the Bell System, a national network, is the largest phone system in the world by far, and probably the most efficient.

The Wright brothers, Wilbur and Orville, demonstrated a workable aircraft at Kitty Hawk, North Carolina, in 1903.

The U.S.A. is famous for gigantic corporations such as Boeing, which sold U.S. $3,300,000,000 worth of aircraft in 1973.
←

of its people, and their ability to make things work on a large scale. For example, the automobile was the result of many efforts, mainly in Europe, but the United States took this invention and developed it into a mass-produced vehicle within the means of most people. Earlier examples were Howe's sewing machine and Whitney's cotton gin, both of which helped to

After a concerted and successful effort to smash the atom and create an atomic bomb during World War II, American scientists turned their attention to making nuclear power available for peaceful pursuits. This is the giant cyclotron developed at the University of California.

Thomas A. Edison (1847–1931) was one of the greatest and most productive inventors of his time. He created the first practical incandescent lamp, developed a complete electrical distribution system for light and power and in 1881–82 the first central electric-light power plant in the world. In the same period he built and operated an experimental electric locomotive that picked up the current from the rails through the wheels. He held over 1,300 patents for products, such as the first successful phonograph and an automatic telegraph.

revolutionize American life—along with vulcanized rubber, the telephone, the electromagnetic telegraph, the passenger elevator, mechanized farm machinery, electric light, and others too numerous to mention.

Steel is basic to American industry. Nearly one fifth of United States steel-making capacity is concentrated within a 50-mile radius of Pittsburgh, Pennsylvania, where the mill above is located.

MANUFACTURING

Coal, from Pennsylvania, West Virginia, and Illinois, and nearby iron ore form the basis for the steel industry, which is located in the heart of the nation. Pittsburgh, Youngstown, Cleveland, Gary, and Chicago are the main steel cities. As the iron ore deposits deteriorated and imports became more important, new steel mills were added on the East coast.

The variety of products manufactured in the Northeast and Midwest is impressive. New England manufactures textiles, leather goods, toys, and machine tools, among other items. Along the Atlantic coast are garment-making, food processing, oil refineries, shipbuilding, and chemicals. Inland, around Chicago and Detroit are manufacturers of automobiles, and rubber products, meat packers, and oil refineries.

Outside of the belt of industry that extends from New York to Chicago are smaller but important manufacturing areas. The Houston-Dallas-Fort Worth area is dominant in the petroleum business. St. Louis is a large trading hub, Minneapolis is known for its flour mills, Los Angeles for its motion picture and television industry, and Seattle for its airplane construction.

AGRICULTURE

The U.S.A. is the most important agricultural country in the world. Four factors make this possible: one half of the country is tillable, the soil is good to excellent, the humid continental and subtropical climates are conducive to growing crops, and modern methods of farming provide efficient operations.

In the northern part of the U.S.A., dairy farms are located near urban areas where milk, butter and cheese are sold. This area has sufficient warmth and rainfall to support hay, corn, oats, and grass pastures. Adjoining the dairying states of the Midwest (Wisconsin is the largest) is the Corn Belt. Here hot days and nights and rich soil produce large crops of corn (maize), some for table use, but mostly for feed for hogs and cattle. Westward are the great wheat plains, producing both spring and winter wheat that supply not only this nation but many other countries of the world. The South, once the

Steam pours out of the cooling towers at Three Mile Island nuclear generating station at Harrisburg, Pennsylvania, one of the plants using atomic energy for peaceful purposes. This is an alternative to the use of fossil fuel for the generation of electric power.

Agriculture is highly mechanized today. This machine is discing (using a disk-harrow) to prepare the ground for planting. Machines such as these make possible the tremendous productivity of America's farmlands.

"land of cotton," now produces tobacco, peanuts, soybeans, and livestock. Citrus fruit is the important produce of Florida, Texas, and California. The Pacific Northwest is the prime forest area of the nation, and supplies much of the building materials.

TRANSPORTATION

A modern economy cannot exist without a good transportation system. Waterways were the most important roads in the U.S.A. until the construction of railways began in the early 1800's. But it was following the War between the States that railway construction began in earnest. Aided by land grants, the railway builders laid tracks across the nation, until a network of connecting lines crisscrossed the land.

Over 300,000 miles (480,000 km.) of track now exist. Competition began later on from trucking, pipelines, and improved waterways and the railways' decline began with the building of many spur lines, and the abandonment of much passenger service. The importance of railways for long distance freight hauling continues, and the welfare of the lines is a grave concern to the nation today. Trucking is heavily regulated by the government to assure fairness of rates.

Modern highways, many paralleling railway tracks, began in the 20th century as the automobile became one of the most important aspects of American life. A network of superhighways was sponsored by state and Federal governments so that long distances can be travelled quickly and in relative safety. In fact,

Modern steel commuter cars are often used for short hauls by the railways. The current energy crisis is helping to revive this industry which had been hard hit by car and air travel.

Containers, containerships and new shipping techniques developed in the U.S.A. to speed cargo to the ports of the world with more safety and security than in the past.

the American highway system is unparalleled in the world. Although air transportation is fully developed and an important part of the economy, the airlines tend to duplicate routes and have run into financial trouble, especially in their overseas operations.

MODERN STRESSES

A highly productive, industrialized economy is not without its problems. The growth of large metropolitan areas is causing stress in the life styles of families. Cars are a necessity, not a luxury, and gasoline supplies are getting scarcer and more expensive all the time. Highways around cities not only are taking rich land from production but are clogged, polluting nightmares during rush hours. The rapid use of natural resources which cannot be replaced is forcing the nation to depend on other countries for imports, oil especially. More importantly, the people are beginning to realize that the rapid rate of resource use cannot continue. This was dramatically demonstrated by the energy

shortage during the winter of 1974. The nation suddenly awoke to the fact that fossil energy is limited and that alternative means must be found. The nation is at decision point. New policies and perhaps new life styles will have to be developed, but this is a nation of optimistic, confident, inventive people who believe in their ability to solve problems.

America is listening. Radar installations are not only being used for research, but for protection. An Early Warning System is in operation to defend against unexpected air attacks.

This scene, published in "Harper's Weekly," shows a group of immigrants entering the port of New York during the 1850's, when the average rate was approximately 235,000 a year. By 1860 about one half of New York City's population was foreign-born. At that time, 200,000 Irish immigrants made New York the largest Irish city in the world.

5. THE PEOPLE

ALTHOUGH the population (212,000,000) of the U.S.A. has a density of 56 per square mile (56 per 2.6 sq. km.), the majority (149,325,000) of the people live in urban areas of over 2,500. The largest concentration is along the East coast which houses over one fourth of the population. Another area that is becoming very densely populated is along the California coastline between the San Diego-Los Angeles region and San Francisco.

In 1910, rural and urban areas were almost equal in population. Today twice as many people live in cities as in farm communities.

No other peoples change homes so frequently. One person in five moves every year, often in the same community, but many from one city or state to another. Thousands of Americans also live outside the country. Another instance of this mobility is that citizens think nothing of commuting 10 to 30 miles (16 to 48 km.) to work and school, drive many miles to go shopping, to visit friends or to seek recreation.

BACKGROUNDS

The diversity of population united into one relatively cohesive society is a striking characteristic of the U.S.A. All Americans are immigrants or descendants of immigrants, including the American Indians who migrated here long ago and who today number 750,000. The pre-Revolutionary population was basically British, with strong admixtures of Germans, French Huguenots and others. This old American stock was the first to push into the Midwest and Southwest after the founding of the Republic. After 1820, it was followed by waves of new immigrants from Europe. The majority of people coming before 1880 were from northwestern Europe. A large number of them were professional people and about 90 per cent could read and write. Although many of them settled in communities of their own, they were similar in culture and belief and easily merged into one society, basically English in its cultural origins. Some of these earlier immigrants whose influ-

An islet in New York Harbor—Ellis Island—served as the main point of reception and processing of immigrants, from 1892 until 1943.

ence still remains are: the Germans of Pennsylvania and the Midwest, the Norwegians and Swedes who settled in Minnesota and that area where pine forests and lakes abound, the Swiss who settled in Wisconsin and made it the cheese capital of America. At an earlier date, a few Spanish had settled the West coast, some French had settled in the New Orleans area, and many blacks were brought as slaves to the South.

After 1880, migration shifted and people

These modern Navajo Indians are descendants of the earliest inhabitants of Monument Valley, which covers several thousand acres in Utah and Arizona. The area is noted for the many red natural sandstone monuments that tower above the valley floor, some reaching as high as 1,000 feet (300 metres).

The first Jews arrived in America before 1650 and have played an important part in the business and intellectual life of the U.S.A. The Touro Synagogue in Newport, Rhode Island, erected in 1763 is the oldest in America and a national historic site.

came from southern and eastern Europe: Austrians, Czechs, Greeks, Italians, Russians, Hungarians, and Poles. Most of these were unskilled workers who took jobs at low pay. Mexicans came to work on the farms of the South and West, Jews fleeing religious persecution arrived in Eastern cities, especially New York, and thousands of Chinese and Japanese moved into the West.

In more recent years, large numbers of people from Caribbean and South American countries have come to the U.S.A., along with some from India, Pakistan and the Philippines.

These immigrants brought with them their languages, religions, and customs, moved into pocket communities in large cities and many still are there, retaining the Old World ways. However, their children grew up as Americans,

with fewer traditions from the Old World. Today, in many parts of the country ethnic groups live together, and are adopting more or less the habits of other groups as well as of the older Americans.

Nationwide, simultaneous broadcasts of radio and television (even the advertising) bring ideas into all the homes and tend to create new standards for the new Americans, in food, music, entertainment, political attitudes and beliefs.

The various immigrant groups have all contributed to the American cuisine, and regional, as apart from ethnic, styles of preparing food survive. New England is still famous for its lobster, clam and fish chowders, codfish cakes, baked beans, boiled dinners, Indian pudding, and Boston brown bread. The South developed a distinctive type of cooking based on

Black descendants of slaves and, more recently, immigrants from Puerto Rico (a Commonwealth of the U.S.A.) had to be assimilated into the huge American melting pot. It became an educational problem. This is a mixed class in a Brooklyn, New York, school.

Many Americans prefer fast food service—short order dishes which are either eaten on the spot or taken out to eat at home.

During the two-week-long celebration of the Mardi Gras in New Orleans, Louisiana, there are torchlight parades, dancing in the streets and costume balls that culminate in the major parade, that of the Krewe of Rex, shown here. It is estimated that a million people throng the parade route each year in mid-February.

pork and chicken, black-eyed peas, hominy (a kind of polenta), mustard greens, sweet potatoes, and cornbread. In the Southwest, the Mexican influence is strong—chili, tacos, enchiladas and refried beans. In the urban and rural pockets where recent immigrant groups keep their identity, Greek, Italian, German, Armenian, Chinese, Japanese, and Central European dishes are served in homes and restaurants.

Over and above all this, the news and publishing media and the development of coast-to-coast distribution systems, including frozen foods and supermarkets, have brought about a blending of many elements. Spaghetti, pizza, lasagna, blintzes, bagels, tacos, chopped chicken liver, codfish cakes and Southern fried chicken are now available in small cities and towns throughout the country, where, a quarter of a century ago, most of them were unknown.

In spite of this, Americans are still heavy consumers of roast beef, hamburgers, hot dogs (frankfurters) and potatoes.

RELIGION

The Constitution gives all people in the country the freedom to worship or not worship as they please. Various Protestant denominations include approximately 70,000,000 people, Roman Catholics 48,000,000, Jews 6,000,000, Eastern Orthodox 3,500,000, Old Catholic and Armenian 800,000, and Buddhists 100,000. There are also many small sects throughout the land, some of which relate to other faiths than

Santa Barbara Mission stands on the heights overlooking the seaside city of Santa Barbara in southern California. It is called "Queen of the Missions" mainly because of its handsome Spanish architecture. The altar light has never gone out during the more than 150 years since the Spanish Franciscan Padres founded the mission.

the ones mentioned previously. The blacks, who are mainly Christians of various denominations, were traditionally segregated, forming their own congregations.

LANGUAGE

The official language of the United States is English, but an English with somewhat different spelling, vocabulary, usage and pronunciation from that of England. American English has evolved over 200 years of independent history, during which it developed a number of distinctive regional variations and enriched its vocabulary with words and expressions derived from Continental European, American Indian, Black American and Hispano-American sources. Unlike England, the U.S.A. has no London-Oxford-Cambridge Establishment to set standards of speech. However, radio, television, films and population mobility are diminishing

regional differences to a marked degree, and the influence of American speech is even strong in England today.

Other languages are spoken in certain regions. About 1,000,000 speakers of a French dialect survive in the State of Louisiana (all but a few speak English also.) In the Southwest, many people speak Spanish—some are descendants of early Spanish settlers, but many more are recent immigrants from Mexico. Spanish is now widely heard in New York City and Miami, due to recent waves of Caribbean immigrants—public schools in New York City even teach in Spanish to accommodate the newcomers.

EDUCATION

A hundred years ago only a few Americans received a formal education. Today the country believes that all Americans, black and white, deserve an opportunity for free education, but

Every June, Harvard alumni flock to Cambridge from all parts of the U.S.A. to help celebrate commencement at the oldest and one of the most prestigious of American universities. Among the speeches that have been delivered at these ceremonies was that of Gen. George Marshall which launched the Marshall Plan that helped rebuild Europe after World War II.

putting this into practice in integrated schools is a continuing problem. The public school system is supported by local and state taxes, to a limited extent by the national government. Both academic and technical schools are available, along with night schools for teenagers, and for adults who work during the day. Private and parochial schools exist all over the nation for those who can afford to take advantage of them. Low-cost schools beyond the 12th grade are offered by many communities so that students do not have to travel far from home. Community junior colleges provide study for the 13th and 14th years.

Most of the states provide universities for higher learning at a lower tuition cost than most private colleges and universities that are abundant throughout the country. A large number of scholarships for college education are made available for worthy but needy students and for athletes. In 1970, some 2,556,000 students took advantage of advanced education. Among these were 135,000 students who came from foreign countries to enter colleges in America. Of these,

35 per cent came from the Far East, 19 per cent Latin American, 15 per cent European, 12 per cent from the Near and Middle East, 11 per cent from countries in North America other than the U.S.A., 6 per cent African and 2 per cent from Oceania.

THE ARTS

Early painters in the U.S.A., such as Gilbert Stuart, famous for his portraits of George Washington, studied in Europe and were influ-

More and more young people are going to vocational schools instead of taking college preparatory courses as the demand for technological skills and services increases in the U.S.A.

and their everyday activities. John Singer Sargent, James McNeill Whistler, and Mary Cassatt, however, were 19th century U.S. painters who worked in Europe. Whistler was famous for his watercolors and etchings, and especially for the portrait of his mother now in the Louvre. Other famous painters include John Steuart Curry, Georgia O'Keeffe and Thomas Hart Benton.

Among recent painters, Jackson Pollock was acclaimed for his abstract works, achieved by dripping paint on a canvas laid flat on the floor, and Andrew Wyeth for his almost photographic realism.

The National Gallery in Washington and the Metropolitan Museum of Art in New York, which contain many American paintings, are among the most complete collections of art in the world.

enced by the schools there. Gradually, artists began to turn away from this influence and portray life in America. George Inness was inspired by the beautiful scenery, Winslow Homer by the sea, Thomas Eakins, and later, George Bellows and Grant Wood, by the people

The National Gallery of Art in Washington, D.C., one of the world's greatest museums, is the gift of Andrew Mellon, and houses his whole collection, as well as other collections of masterpieces of European painting and sculpture.

This dramatic painting, called "Breezing Up," in the National Gallery of Art in Washington, D.C., is typical of the art of Winslow Homer, great American painter of the second half of the 19th century.

Thomas Eakins, who painted this sandlot baseball game, was a specialist in portraying American life of the late 19th and early 20th centuries.

Much American sculpture before World War II was monumental and traditional. The Irish-born Augustus Saint-Gaudens was one of the most famous sculptors—the Adams Monument in Washington and the seated Lincoln in Chicago are two of his works. Daniel Chester French was responsible for the bronze statue in the Lincoln Memorial in Washington, D.C., and the Minuteman at Concord, Massachusetts. The "Fountain of the Great Lakes" in Chicago and the Washington Monument in Seattle, Washington, are two of the works of Lorado Taft. The huge bronze doors at the Capitol building in Washington, as well as the "Armed Liberty" above the dome were designed by Thomas Crawford. Later sculptors turned to abstract forms, notably Alexander Calder, famous for his "mobiles," or moving sculptures, Louise Nevelson, and David Smith.

ARCHITECTURE

America's major contribution to architecture is the skyscraper. Louis H. Sullivan followed the theory that "form follows function." The well designed building has a style and uses materials suited to the purposes of the building. One of the men who adopted this theory was Frank Lloyd Wright who became one of the world's most famous architects. Buckminster Fuller produced such revolutionary concepts as the Dymaxion House and the geodesic dome, the latter widely adopted by U.S. technology.

LITERATURE

The American literary tradition began early in the country's history with Benjamin Franklin, perhaps the best known of 18th-century writers. Washington Irving wrote tales of early New York, and J. Fenimore Cooper was known for tales of the frontier; Edgar Allan Poe wrote poems and short stories which had a great influence in Europe, especially France, and

Henry Wadsworth Longfellow wrote many of his well loved poems in this house, including "The Village Blacksmith" and "The Children's Hour." The Longfellow House is one of many distinguished homes on Brattle Street, Cambridge, Massachusetts.

One of Frank Lloyd Wright's most exciting houses is "Falling Water" at Bear Run in western Pennsylvania. In this house, built in 1936–37, he uses the cantilever principle with great slabs of concrete jutting out over the waterfall to create a spectacular house open to the air and woodland scenery surrounding it.

All large and many small American cities have an art museum, and attendance has risen in the last two decades as people have more leisure. The Albright-Knox Art Gallery in Buffalo, New York, is one of the large ones, with its handsome classical exterior and a notable art collection.

It was in this dignified southern mansion at Bardstown, Kentucky, that Stephen Foster wrote the famous ballad "My Old Kentucky Home." Called Federal Hill, this is one of the most famous houses in the U.S.A. Here, many distinguished men have visited, including four Presidents.

invented the detective story; Ralph Waldo Emerson composed essays, poetry and philosophy. Nathaniel Hawthorne wrote of life in New England, Herman Melville told of the sea ("Moby Dick" was his best known book). Henry James described the discovery of Europe by the American rich and Mark Twain wrote of life on the Mississippi. Famous poets include Walt Whitman, Henry Wadsworth Longfellow, Oliver Wendell Holmes, John Greenleaf Whittier, Emily Dickinson, Robert Frost, Ezra Pound, William Carlos Williams, T.S. Eliot (who became an English citizen), and Edna St. Vincent Millay.

The American novel was developed in the 20th century by a number of influential writers including William Faulkner, who described the rural South, Ernest Hemingway, whose precise prose style had a wide influence, John Steinbeck, who recorded the Depression of the 1930's, and John Dos Passos, whose huge novel *U.S.A.* reflected the changes in American life after World War I. Others were F. Scott Fitzgerald who caught the mood of the 1920's, Gertrude Stein who wrote surrealist prose, and more recently, Norman Mailer, Kurt Vonnegut, John Barth and Thomas Pynchon, whose works reached the younger readers of the 1960's.

Of the playwrights, Eugene O'Neill became the most renowned.

MUSIC

Sentimental songs and traditional English and Irish ballads and folk songs were played by the people in the early years of American history. Stephen Foster, who composed over 200 songs, is known for his American folk music, often based on Negro spirituals. Classical music became popular during the Reconstruction Period. In 1878, the New York Symphony was formed, followed by the Boston Symphony in 1881, and the New York Metropolitan Opera in 1883.

The boy could be "Tom Sawyer" or "Huckleberry Finn," two of the characters created by Samuel Clemens, the American satirist who wrote under the pen name of Mark Twain. His boyhood home (right) at Hannibal, Missouri, is the setting of many incidents in these famous tales. The building to the left is a museum of Twain memorabilia.

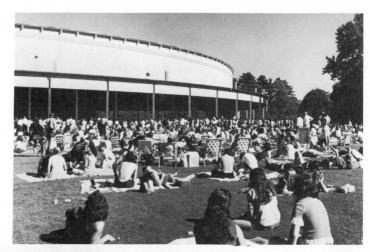

Music lovers listen to a summer concert at Tanglewood, an estate in the blue Berkshire Hills of western Massachusetts. It is now famous as the summer home of the Boston Symphony, its Berkshire Festival, and its unique Berkshire Music Center.

World-famous interpreter of jazz, Duke Ellington, was a major American composer, as well as a pianist and orchestra leader. Here Diahann Carroll, singer-actress, is on the left, and Paula Kelly, dancer-actress, on the right.

The most truly American contribution to music came from New Orleans with the introduction of ragtime and jazz, which were derived from the Negro rhythms of the South. Scott Joplin and William C. Handy were two black composers who were largely responsible for popularizing this type of music. George Gershwin became famous with his "Rhapsody in Blue" and his light opera "Porgy and Bess." Paul Whiteman gave the first jazz concert on a classical stage and later toured the United States and Europe with much success. One of the foremost composers in this vein was Edward Kennedy ("Duke") Ellington.

For two weeks every summer the Hatch Memorial Shell on the bank of the Charles River at Boston, Massachusetts, is the setting for nightly open-air concerts by the Boston Symphony Orchestra, one of the most distinguished American orchestras. In the winter the Orchestra performs at Symphony Hall with "Pops" concerts featuring popular as well as traditional serious music, both classical and modern.

73

The buildings are all modern at Lincoln Center, a cultural and educational complex on Manhattan's upper west side, which includes the Metropolitan Opera House, the New York State Theatre for ballet, musical comedy and opera, the Vivian Beaumont Theatre for drama, and several other theatres as well as the Juilliard School of Music and a library and museum of the performing arts.

Composers of light opera and musical comedy of quality include Sigmund Romberg (Viennese-born), Irving Berlin, Victor Herbert (Dublin-born), Cole Porter and Jerome Kern. Serious musical composers like Aaron Copland, Howard Hanson, Charles Ives and Walter Piston have continued to bring American music to the world.

John Cage, a more recent composer, has startled audiences with his innovations, some of which include noises made with objects other than musical instruments, and some of which include periods of silence.

THEATRE AND CINEMA

Widespread belief that all plays and actors were immoral began with the Puritans. In 1736, the Dock Street Theatre opened in Charleston,

Charlie Chaplin, considered one of the geniuses of the motion picture industry, gained fame as a comedian in the silent movies during the 1920's. He is shown here with Jackie Coogan in "The Kid." With his little black moustache and baggy trousers, he became known throughout the world.

Most movies are now shot on location rather than in the huge Hollywood studios of the Golden Age of the cinema. A typical Western always features a chase and a fight.

S. C., and shortly after, a theatre was begun in Philadelphia. Most of the plays were brought from England. Few theatres existed in the U.S.A. until 1825 but, after this, interest rose until within a few years almost every city of any size boasted a theatre. New York City became the drama capital and still remains so. Stock companies and acting groups tour the country performing in many cities. Community theatres and workshops are available in many places, and summer theatre is fast becoming an important form of entertainment.

One area in which the U.S.A. lags behind some European countries is government subsidizing of the performing arts. Although there is a recently created National Endowment for the Arts in Washington, there is nothing to compare with the national theatres, operas and ballets in England, Denmark or France.

The motion picture, developed by Thomas Edison, was first shown in 1889 in houses called nickelodeons, packed with people eager to see this new form of entertainment. By 1927, when the first talkie, "The Jazz Singer," was released there were over 20,000 large movie houses across the land. The 30's and 40's were banner decades in movie production, but today costs have made the large lots impossible to keep up.

President Franklin D. Roosevelt in the 1930's was the first to use radio to get his message to the people in "fireside chats." Today, political figures count on television to project their image to the public.

While Hollywood still produces movies for the entire world it does so mostly for television.

Today, almost every citizen has easy access to a television set, and can view the best and worst of theatre, movies and music. Radio, popular in the days just before television, has become entertainment for travelling and for enthusiasts of "hi-fi."

Many blacks have risen recently to the top in baseball and other sports, such as football and basketball. Although they have for a long time been well accepted in the field of entertainment, especially in popular music, it took much manoeuvering before blacks got equal treatment in the big leagues. Only in 1974 did a black first get appointed to manage a baseball club.

The phonograph record business supplies not only the U.S.A. but the whole world with the latest in American-style popular music.

SPORTS AND RECREATION

America is sports mad, as people have more leisure due to a shorter work week and earlier retirement.

Baseball may be known as "the national sport," but in many areas football, both pro-

Football, with its intricate formations and plays which require split-second timing, provides crowds with constant action. Professional football has more efficient players, but college football is more spirited. The quarterback here from Pennsylvania State University, a land-grant college, is hiding the ball before handing it off to one of his halfbacks.

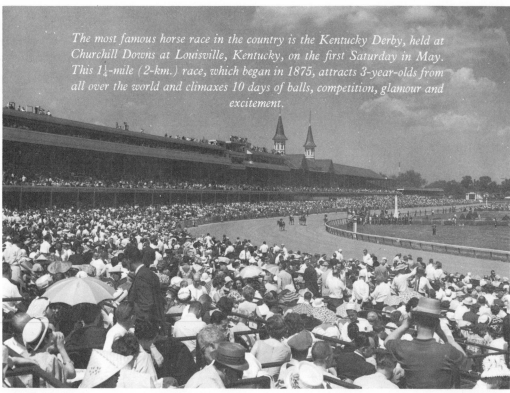

The most famous horse race in the country is the Kentucky Derby, held at Churchill Downs at Louisville, Kentucky, on the first Saturday in May. This 1¼-mile (2-km.) race, which began in 1875, attracts 3-year-olds from all over the world and climaxes 10 days of balls, competition, glamour and excitement.

fessional and amateur, and basketball are drawing larger crowds. Spectators spend millions of dollars each year following their favorite sports in stadiums as well as on television. Leading the list are the three major sports but there are many fans for watching tennis, golf, boxing and horse-racing.

Participant sports are led by golf and tennis, with fishing, swimming, skiing, boating, bicycling, camping and hunting following more or less in that order.

At one time the only place a man or woman, boy or girl, could find a gym to work out in was at the YMCA or YWCA. Today the U.S.A. is full of health clubs, swimming pools, bowling alleys, and gyms, which have sprung up even in the smallest rural communities. Modern tech-

nology has made it possible to use ski and sled slopes, and ice skating rinks for most of the winter months. The majority of public and private schools require some type of physical

Fishing is a big sport all over the U.S.A. This fisherman is pulling a trout out of one of Colorado's snow-fed streams. This state with glacial mountain scenery, keeps its 1,400 streams, 2,000 high-altitude lakes and 62 warm-water reservoirs stocked with over 24,000,000 trout and other fish.

With sail furled, a single-masted ketch rides at anchor in Edgartown Harbor, one of the boating ports on Martha's Vineyard Island off the coast of Cape Cod, Massachusetts. Edgartown Light is in the background. Martha's Vineyard and nearby Nantucket are popular island summer resorts.

education. The U.S.A. does not have a formal national sports organization, yet it has always fielded a representative team of amateurs for Olympic world events.

More and more people are slanting their recreation to the Arts and Crafts. The urge to "do one's own thing" has caught on with adults and young people, so that today the U.S.A. is becoming a nation of "Do It Yourselfers."

TOURISM

Tourism within the U.S.A. is highly developed—but until recently it was geared mainly to accommodating native and Canadian tourists. Relatively few people from other

In the winter in the northern states and in the Rockies and Sierras, skiers flock to the slopes in larger numbers than ever before.

When a tourist first sights Miami Beach, Florida, from the air, the long string of hotels on the narrow white sands, all reflecting the bright sun, compose a scene that is never forgotten.

continents came to the U.S.A. as tourists—especially when compared to the huge numbers of American pleasure-seekers who went abroad. With shifts in the value of the dollar and the growth of a prosperous middle class in Western Europe and Japan, the situation changed, and the late 1960's saw swarms of foreign tourists visiting the U.S.A. Most American tourist facilities, however, are still far from duplicating the efforts made in some other countries, notably in the area of providing personnel who speak other languages than English.

INDEX

80